Two Dollar Radio

VEGAN
COOKING

Recipes, Stories Behind the Recipes,
and Inspiration for Vegan Cheffing.

Two Dollar Radio
Books too loud to Ignore

WHO WE ARE TWO DOLLAR RADIO is a family-run outfit dedicated to reaffirming the cultural and artistic spirit of the publishing industry. We aim to do this by presenting bold works of literary merit, each book, individually and collectively, providing a sonic progression that we believe to be too loud to ignore.

TwoDollarRadio.com

Proudly based in

Columbus
OHIO

@TwoDollarRadio

@TwoDollarRadio

/TwoDollarRadio

ALL PHOTOS, ART, RECIPES, AND TEXT → Eric Obenauf

PHOTO, P. 17 → David Berkowitz, https://www.flickr.com/photos/davidberkowitz/6348507490/

Two Dollar Radio
HEADQUARTERS

^ *Exterior of Two Dollar Radio Headquarters, 2019.*

COME VISIT US IN BEAUTIFUL COLUMBUS, OHIO!

Two Dollar Radio Headquarters is a bar, café, plant-based watering hole, and bookstore specializing in the best in independently published literature.

TwoDollarRadioHQ.com	@TwoDollarHQ
@TwoDollarRadioHQ	/TwoDollarRadioHQ

Punk Rock

Converting to Metrics

VOLUME MEASUREMENT CONVERSIONS

U.S.	METRIC
¼ teaspoon	1.25 ml
½ teaspoon	2.5 ml
¾ teaspoon	3.75 ml
1 teaspoon	5 ml
1 tablespoon	15 ml
¼ cup	62.5 ml
½ cup	125 ml
¾ cup	187.5 ml
1 cup	250 ml

WEIGHT MEASUREMENT CONVERSIONS

U.S.	METRIC
1 ounce	28.4 g
8 ounces	227.5 g
16 ounces (1 pound)	455 g

COOKING TEMPERATURE CONVERSIONS

To convert temperatures in Fahrenheit to Celsius, subtract 32 and multiply by . 5556 (or $\frac{5}{9}$): $\mathbf{C = (°F - 32) \times \frac{5}{9}}$

EXAMPLE: $(350°F - 32) \times \frac{5}{9} = 176.667°C$

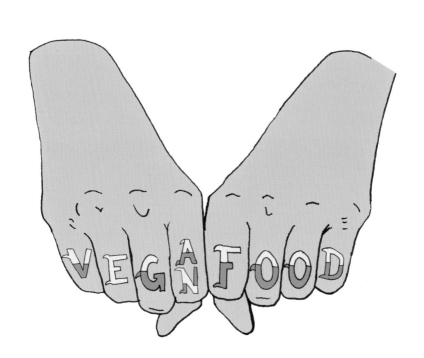

TABLE OF CONTENTS

---

1   This is a very important chapter, maybe the most important.
2   This chapter begins to tie it all together; practice patience and discernment in equal measure.
3   This chapter is when we achieve a dramatic crescendo; the Vegan Hunger Demons have been confronted and appropriately slayed.
4   This chapter is really important, too, and also maybe tied for the most important as it is foundational.

Introduction

When I was a five-year-old kid growing up in Sheboygan, my favorite meal was smashed sweet potato with melted vegan cheddar cashew cheeze, charred root, and candied walnuts with a rosemary-thyme garnish. My Uncle Gary used to say while I was stuffing my face, "Randall, food doesn't just happen." Thirty-three years later and I can tell you this with absolute certainty and the conviction of my office: my Uncle Gary was right.

Food begins as seeds in gardens. Nurtured by the elements, it then grows to sustain life. *Our lives.* Food is cosmic, if cosmic meant something more tethered to earth.

My Uncle Gary never said it, but I would also posit — here, now, publicly, but also in my forthcoming TED talk — that food is a story. And that is the story of the farmers who harvested the vegetables, the delivery truck drivers who disseminated (not a dirty word) those vegetables, the chefs who prepared those vegetables into delectable (also not a dirty word) meals, and the diners fortunate enough to savor those meals. It is the story of life. Their lives.

However, we don't have time for any of that here. This is the story of myself and my good friend, Speed Dog. How we made a menu of delectable (see note above about not a dirty word), mouth-watering vegan food and how it ruled. This is also the story behind the stories about how those menu items were named, thereby crowning them with mythic status.

We serve many of these dishes (or have served many of these dishes) at Two Dollar Radio Headquarters, a bookstore and plant-based watering hole in scenic Columbus, Ohio.

Vive la revolution,
—Jean-Claude van Randy

Handwritten on a coarse piece of utility paper in a remote cabin outside of Zion, November 6, 2019.

Editor's Note About Accessibility of the Recipes

The editors would like to acknowledge that not everyone has an industrial-sized kitchen at their disposal with hard-to-find spices and rare ingredients. The goal with the recipes presented in this *Guide to Vegan Cooking*, was to make them accessible for cheffing in a home kitchen.

Editor's Note on Point of View

In obtaining a consistency amongst the stories contained in this *Guide to Vegan Cooking*, Speed Dog relayed his account of events by writing in the first-person point of view, while Randy offered his by Dictaphone audiocassette in the third-person.

To assemble the stories and diverging view points, we hired a non-partisan court stenographer with very credible references. What remains is a third-person recounting.

"Poets utter great and wise things which they do not themselves understand."
　　—PLATO

"If I go to a dance and I don't sit down, I am dangerous."
　　—CONROY SMITH, "DANGEROUS"

A Note About How Good Cheeze Is

A common lamentation amongst vegans and those looking to make the leap to a vegan diet is how hard it is to give up cheese. *Same!*

One of the first challenges Randy and Speed Dog set for themselves — their Mount Everest, so to speak — was to craft dairy-free cheeses.

After a seared eyebrow, more than one sleepless nights, a blender upgrade, and a bruised trachea resulting from a hot yoga mishap, thus was born *cheeze* with a "z."

CHEEZE

The Deeper the
the Uglier the

Scallion Cheddar Cheeze Spread — p. 14

Buffalo Mac & Cheeze
Buffalo queso tossed with penne and baked.

BUFFALO QUESO

THE DISH: You can, and should, put this buffalo queso on everything. It's like Batman's utility belt, but vegan.

Tofu

RECIPE

1 cup cashews
½ 8-ounce block tofu
Salt + pepper to taste
¾ cup Frank's Red Hot
1½ tablespoons smoked paprika
1 cup nutritional yeast
¾ cup soy milk
⅓ cup olive oil
1 head of garlic

CHEFFING INSTRUCTIONS

- Soak the cashews in hot water for at least 15 minutes.
- Add ingredients to a blender and blend until smooth.
- Garnish with vegan bacon or diced scallions or both!

PAIRING SUGGESTIONS

Toss buffalo queso with noodles for buffao mac & cheeze.
Use buffalo queso on tacos and nachos, drizzle on pizzas,
or just warm and use as a dip with chips.

SCALLION CHEDDAR CHEEZE SPREAD

THE DISH: If Pimento Cheeze is North Florida in summer, this Scallion Cheddar Cheeze Spread pairs well with John Cusack Weather (fall in the Midwest).

RECIPE

1 cup cashews
½ cup nutritional yeast
½ cup vegan mayo (see recipe on p. 114)
½ block tofu
¼ cup plant-based milk
4–6 scallions
Salt + pepper to taste

CHEFFING INSTRUCTIONS

• Soak the cashews in hot water for at least 15 minutes.
• Cut the scallions and divide into white parts and green bits.
• Add ingredients (including scallion whites) to a blender and blend until smooth.
• Garnish with scallion greens.

PAIRING SUGGESTIONS

Vegan meats, such as pepperoni or greasy burgers.
John Cusack movies.
The sound of crunching leaves in the fall.

Carrot Lox Tacos
Carrot lox, scallion cheddar cheeze spread, red beet slaw,
capers, cucumbers, and ranch dressing on a corn tortilla.

The Origin Story

One is not simply born a Jean-Claude; one must become a Jean-Claude. The title is earned.

No, Jean-Claude van Randy was born with an unassuming name (Randall) in an unassuming city (Sheboygan, Wisconsin 53081). He had a bike with a kickstand and liked to race his friends from the cul-de-sac to the fancy, "uppity" stoplight of Lincoln Boulevard. He infrequently won.

Randall was an awkward teen, with braces that sliced his lips, and a mustache. He managed to talk his mother into letting him get an ill-advised nose-ring. (It is worth noting that these are the appearances but not the true soul of his character. Randall was, and still is, a romantic. He could look up at the moon in the night sky and his mind would fill to the brim with haikus, some of which he said aloud, but more often than not he stored within the lock-box of his heart.)

Post community college, post failed-career-as-a-telemarketer, post semi-successful-career-as-a-Yelp-brand-strategist, Randall was floundering. Sheboygan had boxed him in. When he randomly applied for a credit card and received a higher-than-expected credit allowance (a typo on behalf of the bank; whoops!), he absconded from Sheboygan. He packed his bags and left the cul-de-sac, went straight through the fancy, "uppity" stoplight at Lincoln Boulevard and kept on going.

Forty-five minutes later, Randall found himself at a bus stop on the outskirts of Sheboygan. There was one of those strip malls that looks devoid of purpose, but discreetly houses an unmarked Chinese food buffet and a driver's license bureau. Sandwiched between the two was a sandwich board, and on that plastic sandwich board was taped a picture of Jean-Claude van Damme, circa *Hard Target*. It was a film that Randall knew well.

The sandwich board with the picture promised but one thing: Immortality.

Randall was, to say the least, intrigued. His next fateful step was toward the martial arts studio. He never looked back.

Two and a half days later he emerged with a maxed-out credit card, an embossed certificate that he would later frame, a sense of purpose, the seeds of a Kentucky waterfall, and a splashy new title: Jean-Claude van Randy. ∎

Photographic example of what passes
for food in Sheboygan, WI, 2007.

Cheeze Plate
Sliced smoky mozzarella cheeze
with apples and pepitas.

SMOKY MOZZARELLA CHEEZE

THE DISH: This is a solid all-purpose, sliceable (!) cheeze that you can chuck on everything from pizzas (it melts!) to Tortugas to sandwiches.

RECIPE

1 cup cashews
½ cup refined coconut oil
½ cup tapioca flour
2 tablespoons nutritional yeast
3 tablespoons kappa carrageenan
2½ tablespoons lemon juice
3 teaspoons salt
1 tablespoon apple cider vinegar
2 pieces garlic
1 teaspoon onion powder
1 teaspoon liquid smoke
3 cups boiling water

CHEFFING INSTRUCTIONS

• Soak the cashews in hot water for at least 15 minutes.
• Add all ingredients to a blender and blend thoroughly.
• The mixture will thicken along the outside of the blender and you'll notice air bubbles rising in the center, signifying that it's blended.
• Quickly transfer to a container that will be easy to remove cheeze block from, and refrigerate.

The Second Time That Randy Almost Met Speed Dog

It was a sunny day in Sheboygan; the birds cooed in trees.

Randy was celebrating his embossed certificate and new title at one of his favorite plant-based watering holes: Tofu Daddy's Nacho Emporium. Now that he was a freshly minted Jean-Claude and no longer just any old Randall, he had a hard time visiting some of his previous haunts. Folks were transfixed by his raw animal magnetism; many more were in awe of the spiritual balance he now harnessed as a Jean-Claude. Tofu Daddy and his bar-hands always treated Randy A1 since day 1.

Randy stood chatting with Tofu Daddy by the cashew cheeze buffet.

"Beautiful day outside, isn't it?"

"Did you see the birds cooing in the trees?"

A scrappy lad ambled near, biting into a Ring Pop.

"Hey," Tofu Daddy shrieked. "No outside food or drinks allowed!"

Rather than cede a good Ring Pop, the lad bolted, causing a ruckus and then a hullabaloo; in the melee, someone spilled their plate of zesty nachos onto the floor.

"We call those Floor Nachos now," Tofu Daddy said, chuckling in admiration of his own humor.

"Keep your Floor Nachos," Randy said. "I never turn my back on your Buffalo Mac." He ladled some of Tofu Daddy's world-famous gluten-free Buffalo Mac & Cheeze onto his wanting plate.

It would be weeks before Randy met the scrappy lad with the Ring Pop who would become his future trusted and forever pal, Speed Dog. ■

APPS, SALADS & SMALL PLATES

Calgary Carrot Lox Salad — p. 31

Game-Day Chick'n Wangs
Chick'n Wangs tossed in barbecue sauce,
with a side of street sauce for dunking.

GAME-DAY CHICK'N WANGS

THE DISH: This chick'n recipe is pretty solid. Use it to form larger patties if you don't want to mess with the lil' wangs, but adjust bake-time based on thickness.

RECIPE

4 pieces garlic
1½ cups hot water
1 teaspoon onion powder + salt + pepper
1 tablespoon smoked paprika
1 tablespoon oregano
1½ tablespoons mustard

2 cups beans (preferably a non-obtrusive white bean)
2½ cups wheat gluten
2 tablespoons nutritional yeast
1 tablespoon curry
1 tablespoon chili powder

CHEFFING INSTRUCTIONS

• Add everything to blender except wheat gluten and pulverize.
• Add wheat gluten to mixing bowl, and pour on blender ingredients. Stir contents, and knead until everything is combined.
• Pour barbecue sauce on baking pan, and separate chick'n into wang-sized morsels and place on baking pan. Top with barbecue sauce.
• Bake at 400° for ~20 minutes (depending on the size of the wangs).
• In a mixing bowl, add ~2 cups of flour, 2 teaspoons salt, and 2 teaspoons smoked paprika. Stir in a lager with the flour until resembles pancake batter.
• Dip baked wangs in batter and fry in a pan with oil.
• Toss fried wangs in barbecue or hot sauce and win the Big Game!

TATER TOTS

THE DISH: Being based in Columbus, the yoga studio of the Midwest, we needed to get intimate with tots: toss 'em in hot sauce, throw 'em in a casserole, roll 'em in a taco — IDGAF, it's all tasty.

RECIPE

6–7 "A"-sized potatoes
½ cup flour
2 teaspoons onion powder
2 teaspoons salt
1 teaspoon pepper
1 teaspoon smoked paprika
1 teaspoon dill
2 tablespoons fresh parsley

CHEFFING INSTRUCTIONS

- Peel the potatoes and boil for ~10 minutes.
- Allow the potatoes to cool before grating.
- Add potatoes to a mixing bowl with ingredients and knead together by hand, slowly adding flour until mixture achieves desired consistency.
- Form into tot-shaped logs and fry in oil.

PAIRING SUGGESTIONS

Any sandwich ever imagined.

After frying, douse the tots in hot sauce and bake for a few minutes, then dip into farmhouse ranch dressing and live forever.

Tater Tots!

Calgary Carrot Lox Salad
(or, Speed Dog's Reunion with a Feisty Pack Burro)

Speed Dog is the drummer in the band. He's also the driver. It was outside Banff when the tour van — a 1988 Aerostar, gray with a svelte maroon racing stripe — sputtered. Ordinarily the steed galloped down the highways and bi-ways of North America like shimmering quicksilver, but not today. No, not today.

While a mechanic in Calgary's suburbs tended to the Aerostar's wounds and Randy visited an ashram, Speed Dog took a Lime scooter into the city proper. In the distance, he spied Old Goat Mountain, a peak he had summited in his younger days. That fateful summer, he had arrived in Banff with not more than a feisty pack burro named Wanda, a sack of cherry Ring Pops, and a handkerchief; he left Banff a man. As he stood on the peak of Old Goat Mountain, surveying the distance and the great beyond, Speed Dog let out a wild mountain yawp. It echoed into the distance. The moment was eternal and transcendent.

As Speed Dog raced into downtown Calgary, the Lime scooter slowly yawned to a stop. It was not his day for mechanized travel. He was hungry, and sick of the slimy portabella mushroom cap burgers and hummus he so often was stuck eating while out on the dusty trail.

Speed Dog often thought that there are few things in life more transcendent than a solid A+ drum solo. One of them would have to be a roll in the hay with a good salad. As Speed Dog crunched on a transcendent Calgary Cobb Salad on the veranda of a plant-based watering hole, a wet muzzle nudged his forearm. It had been nearly fifteen years since they'd last seen one another, but cherry Ring Pops give Speed Dog a distinguishable scent, one that Wanda recalled to this day. In Speed Dog's jubilation at their reunion, Wanda stole his salad. ■

Calgary Carrot Lox Salad
Lettuce tossed in farmhouse ranch dressing, topped with cucumbers, carrot lox, pickled onions, capers, shredded mozzarella cheeze, and coarse ground black pepper.

CALGARY CARROT LOX SALAD

THE DISH: We've thrown this flavorful Carrot Lox on everything from bagels to tacos, but its smoky taste packs a punch on a salad.

SMOKY CARROT LOX RECIPE

½ teaspoon oregano
1 teaspoon diced garlic
2 teaspoons apple cider vinegar

4 large carrots, peeled
2 tablespoons liquid smoke
1 tablespoon oil
2 teaspoons onion powder

CHEFFING INSTRUCTIONS

• Toss the peeled carrots in oil and salt and bake until soft and able to insert a toothpick or knife easily.
• Allow the carrots to cool, then slice at a 45° angle.
• Place carrots in deep pan and add rest of ingredients, then fill to top with water and let sit for 2–4 hours or overnight before serving.

ASSEMBLY

Nothing's worse than dry lettuce, so we toss the greens in farmhouse ranch dressing, then top with carrot lox, shredded cheeze, capers, coarse ground pepper, pickled onions, and ring with cucumber halves.

PAIRING SUGGESTIONS

A fine merlot or a dunkel.
This is a light vacation lunch, best served on a patio in the shade.

TACOS HERMANOS

THE DISH: Wasn't a joke when we said buffalo queso makes a splash on everything from tacos to sandwiches. This is our staple taco, and it's consistent AF.

SEASONED "BEEF" RECIPE

2 cups textured vegetable protein (TVP)
½ tablespoon each of chili powder and liquid smoke
1 teaspoon each: salt, pepper, crushed red pepper, onion powder
2 tablespoons crushed tomatoes
1½ cups hot water

CHEFFING INSTRUCTIONS

• Add the TVP to a bowl with spices, then hot water and stir.
• Warm corn tortillas in a pan until flexible and soft.

ASSEMBLY

Spread buffalo queso on the tortilla, top with seasoned "beef," then add slaw (see recipe on p. 117), salsa (see recipe on p. 115), aioli (see recipe on p. 114), and pickled onions (see recipe on p. 118).

PAIRING SUGGESTIONS

"Dangerous," by Conroy Smith.
Soggy board-shorts and iced hibiscus tea.

Tacos Hermanos
Seasoned "beef," buffalo queso, slaw, salsa, aioli, and pickled onions on a corn tortilla.

Not Even Lake Erie Perch Fishless Tacos
Fishless filets, buffalo queso, red beet slaw, lemon-pepper aioli,
salsa, chimichurri, and pickled onion.

NOT EVEN LAKE ERIE PERCH FISHLESS TACOS

THE DISH: A solid A+ drum solo, these fish tacos will trigger the sound of flip-flops spanking sand-dimpled heels, and scratchy salsa music trumpeting from an old boombox.

FISHLESS FILET RECIPE

~1 cup plant-based milk
of your choosing
~½ cup lemon juice
1 tablespoon caper juice

1 eggplant, peeled
zest of 1 lemon
1 tablespoon salt
1 teaspoon creole seasoning
~2 cups flour

CHEFFING INSTRUCTIONS

- Peel the eggplant and slice top-to-bottom into long strips.
- Add flour, spices, milk, caper and lemon juice to mixing bowl and stir. Add water slowly until it resembles a thick pancake batter.
- Coat eggplant in batter and fry in pan.

ZESTY

ASSEMBLY

For these tacos, we combine the fishless filets with buffalo queso, slaw, a citrus aioli, salsa, chimichurri, and pickled onions. Chef's kiss!

PAIRING SUGGESTIONS

Put these fishless filets on burritos, tacos, or serve as fish & chips. A cheap, crisp lager and a game of horseshoes.

Not Even Lake Erie Perch Fishless Tacos

Mitch McConnell is mega-old, but that doesn't mean that all old people are deviants. Take Speed Dog's Aunt Louise.

A gentle spirit if ever there was one, Louise is the owner/operator of the *Lake Erie Weekly Herald*, a print newspaper dishing on all things Cleveland, Geneva-on-the-Lake, and Upper Ashtabula. A drummer herself, Louise toured North America with none other than Gordon Lightfoot on his "Summertime Dream" tour, and taught Speed Dog how to keep a beat on a set of upturned pots.

Dissimilar to some of her generation who had a hard time jiving with the plant-based gravy, Louise could understand why Speed Dog would be vegan. She lived for 18 months on a commune in Virginia that made tofu, and in the winter, Louise sits in a rocking chair by a claw-foot wood stove and knits rainbow-colored hammocks. But the one thing Louise struggled to forsake in her own diet at this stage of her life (based equal parts on geography, reading habits, and a boorish general practitioner with an underbite) was seafood. Specifically: Lake Erie perch.

Louise read articles about the health benefits of fish in *TV Guide*; while she wasn't a fisherwoman herself, she enjoyed the

Norman Rockwell-picturesque of the pre-teens in her neighborhood biking to the pier with their fishing rods angled skyward.

"Not even Lake Erie perch?" she asked Speed Dog often.

Speed Dog was not born a kitchen guy the same way that Bob Ross was not born a painter. What I'm talking about here are two things: Craftsmanship, and The Muse.

With Aunt Louise and Lake Erie perch as his muse, Speed Dog crafted his own riff on fish tacos one evening in Geneva-on-the-Lake. It had been a while since he and Randy had found a decent plant-based watering hole, and Speed Dog was excited to be in a full-sized kitchen and not crouched over the 1988 Aerostar touring van's hot plate.

Louise had a rustic A-frame on the coastline with a wraparound porch and 4-person hot tub. Randy was in the lotus position, meditating on a narrow dock. Speed Dog knew better than to disrupt him while he was finding inner balance, even if it was supper time.

Louise looked skeptical as she eyed the tacos, and why wouldn't she? Here's someone who grew up going to all-you-can-eat perch buffets and fish fries at the Catholic church, and not cause she was hip to the religious gravy; she went cause her religion was small white fried fish with an unhealthy amount of tartar sauce. But Louise loved her nephew Speed Dog, and for him she was willing to give his vegan fish tacos a chance.

Lake Erie ♡

She dabbed her chops with a napkin.

Speed Dog waited; he added some hot sauce to his taco and took a gulp of the finest Upper Ashtabula craft beer Louise had purchased, to fill the silence.

"Now that's a solid A+ drum solo," Louise said, pointing a fork at Speed Dog.

It was so good, in fact, that the next morning Louise took leftovers into the *Lake Erie Weekly Herald* office, where she shared the Not Even Lake Erie Perch Fishless Tacos with her assistant editor, Denny, and new marketing manager, Rach.

Louise left the tacos on the community table without an introduction other than allergy information (gluten-free/nut-free/soy-free/vegan), but it was no more than fifteen minutes before Rach and Denny were at her office door. A gob of vegan farmhouse ranch dressing dotted Denny's khaki travel-vest.

"Denny and I have been talking," Rach said. She was prone to hyperbole and was born a millennial, so she had ideas. And opinions.

"The paper has been struggling," Rach said, which was no surprise. Its core demographic were boomers and older-than-boomers, which was why Louise had brought on Rach as her new hotshot marketing manager from Brooklyn. "One of the ways we might expand readership is to appeal to additional demographics rather than just old people."

Louise waited, not thrilled to hear her new marketing manager dismiss their entire readership as "old people." She looked to Denny: nothing. There was also a dollop of vegan farmhouse ranch in his push-broom moustache.

Rach made her two hands into a triangle and paced the room. She had on a black faux-leather jacket, black jeans, and black boots; Louise had never seen her dressed differently. She had black aviator sunglasses clipped to the neckline of her black shirt.

"According to *Forbes*, the number of people who eat a vegan diet in the United States grew by 600%, while *The Economist* declared that 2019 is the year that veganism goes mainstream. Not to mention social media influencers like Alexandria Ocasio-Cortez citing a vegan diet as one of the best ways for individuals to personally combat climate change."

Louise was waiting for the punchline. Obviously, there had to be more to Rach's pitch than ticking off statistics of a vegan diet.

"And that doesn't count alternative lifestyles," Rach continued. "I'm talking health-minded people, like those who may not identify as vegan but do yoga, or run half-marathons and put those 13.1 bumper stickers on their Subaru."

"What are you proposing?" Louise chimed in.

"What I'm proposing is —" Rach leaned forward onto Louise's editor's desk. "Giving Speed Dog and Randy their own column in the *Weekly Herald*. The focus would be on vegan cooking, sure, but it would also include the guys' colorful personalities. I haven't seen Speed Dog so much as eat a salad without telling a story about his summer in Banff, or Randy talk about vegan macaroni and cheeze without digressing into the second time he and Speed Dog almost met. There's lit-er-a-lly nothing like it."

Denny cleared his throat. "I'd liken it to Anthony Bourdain's *Parts Unknown*, but with a hardcore punk rock vegan bent. And if Anthony Bourdain was actually two people. And maybe played by LaKeith Stanfield and Paul Rudd."

Rach shot Denny a look; he quickly apologized.

Louise peered out the window at the skyline of Upper Ashtabula, then to her assistant editor.

"While there's technically something like it," Denny said, "I do believe it's a strong proposal."

And with that, Jean-Claude van Randy and Speed Dog added a new title to their already illustrious names: Columnists at the *Lake Erie Weekly Herald*. ∎

BRUNCH

(No) Crab Cakes Benedict — p. 46

Loaded Breakfast Tortuga
Tofu scramble, cheeze, coconut bacon, and jalapeños
stuffed in a flour tortilla and baked to crispy perfection.

LOADED BREAKFAST TORTUGA

THE DISH: You can legit put anything in a Tortuga. All you gotta do is heat whatever you plan on stuffing inside, then fold into a flour tortilla and bake until golden on the outside. Top this Breakfast Tortuga with a creamy hollandaise sauce for total brunch fulfillment.

TOFU SCRAMBLE RECIPE

1 pack extra firm tofu
¼ cup nutritional yeast
¼ teaspoon curry powder
¼ teaspoon smoked paprika
1 teaspoon salt (taste, and add more if necessary)
¼ tablespoon Worcestershire
½ teaspoon pepper

CHEFFING INSTRUCTIONS

- Add tofu block to mixing bowl.
- Add spices, knead by hand like mixing pizza dough until uniform.

HOLLANDAISE SAUCE RECIPE

3 tablespoons vegan butter or oil
2 tablespoons flour
¼ teaspoon turmeric
1 cup soy milk
2 teaspoons lemon juice
1 tablespoon nutritional yeast
½ teaspoon garlic powder
½ teaspoon salt

CHEFFING INSTRUCTIONS

- Heat oil in pot, then add flour and spices.
- Slowly add milk and stir.

Fully-Loaded

(NO) CRAB CAKES BENEDICT

THE DISH: Pinkies up for this one! These buttery (no) crab cake patties are certain to delight your Pinochle crew. You can also serve these crabby patties as appetizers with a citrus aioli, or on a sandwich.

CRABBY PATTIES RECIPE

2 cans jackfruit
⅛ cup capers
¼ cup caper juice
½ cup grated carrot
¼ onion, diced
1 teaspoon cajun seasoning

1½ cups corn,
    pureed with 3 pieces of garlic
½ tablespoon seaweed spice
2 tablespoons lemon juice
~2 cups breadcrumbs

CHEFFING INSTRUCTIONS

- Add jackfruit to pot, discard cores of pieces and pull until stringy. Add capers, seaweed spice, lemon juice, and caper juice and simmer so that jackfruit absorbs flavor.
- Blend corn and garlic.
- Combine jackfruit, corn puree, diced onion and carrot, and breadcrumbs to a mixing bowl and stir until achieves consistency of a semi-firm patty.

ASSEMBLY

Heat both sides of patty in pan with light oil, add to toasted english muffin half, and top with hollandaise sauce (see recipe on p. 45).

JACKFRUIT

(No) Crab Cakes Benedict
(No) crab cakes on toast, topped with
tofu scramble and hollandaise sauce.

Everything (but the bagel) Carrot Lox Wrap
Carrot lox, scallion cheddar cheeze, lettuce, capers,
cucumbers, farmhouse ranch in a baked tortilla
topped with everything-bagel seasoning.

EVERYTHING (BUT THE BAGEL) CARROT LOX WRAP

THE DISH: This is a staple in our pantry, and we use it to add a jolt of flavor to everything from boring, plain burger buns to wraps.

EVERYTHING-BAGEL SEASONING RECIPE

1 tablespoon poppy seeds
1 tablespoon sesame seeds
1 tablespoon black sesame seeds
1 tablespoon salt
1 tablespoon minced dried onion

CHEFFING INSTRUCTIONS

• Add all the spices to a spice shaker with larger holes and shake until mixed.

ASSEMBLY

• Wrap the smoky carrot lox (see recipe on p. 31), lettuce, capers, salsa or tomatoes, cheeze, cucumbers and farmhouse ranch dressing in a tortilla.
• Spray the outside of the tortilla with cooking spray and sprinkle wtih everything-bagel seasoning.
• Bake in the oven until toasted.

PAIRING SUGGESTIONS

Sprinkle seasoning on everything from tacos to mac & cheeze.
A stroll down to the harbah to get some chowdah.

BREAKFAST TACOS

THE DISH: A smoky bacon can be a great addition to any breakfast dish, to garnish casseroles, or to add a crunch to a salad.

COCONUT BACON RECIPE

1 cup coconut flakes
1 tablespoon maple syrup
1 teaspoon smoked paprika
¼ teaspoon liquid smoke
1 teaspoon pepper
1 tablespoon oil

CHEFFING INSTRUCTIONS

• Add coconut flakes and oil to a warm pan.
• Add spices to the coconut flakes and stir constantly.
• Heat until coconut bacon is no longer soft, but crisp.

ASSEMBLY

• Heat corn tortillas in a pan until pliable and warm.
• Sauté the tofu scramble (see recipe on p. 45) in a pan, and add to tortillas.
• Top with slaw, salsa, coconut bacon, shredded cheeze, street sauce (see recipe on p. 87).

PAIRING SUGGESTIONS

Use as a fixin' on a burger, or as a garnish.
Grapefruit mimosas at brunch.

Breakfast Tacos
Tofu scramble, slaw, salsa, coconut bacon, shredded cheeze, and street sauce.

Breakfast Sando
Chickpea scramble with sausage, tomato, jalapeño, and hollandaise sauce on a bun.

BREAKFAST SANDO

THE DISH: Some folks just don't do soy, so it's good to have a go-to breakfast option other than tofu scramble. These chickpea patties can be somewhat dense and dry, so we tend to top them with tomatoes, jalapeños, slaw, or hollandaise sauce for an added bit of moisture.

CHICKPEA SCRAMBLE RECIPE

2 cups chickpea flour
¼ cup diced cilantro
2 tablespoons nutritional yeast
½ teaspoon curry powder
1 teaspoon salt + pepper
½ cup garbanzo beans
1½ cups aquafaba
½ teaspoon oregano

HARDCORE
PADDLE-BOARD
SESH

CHEFFING INSTRUCTIONS

• Combine all ingredients in mixing bowl and stir.
• Either bake these patties in the oven at 350° for ~7 minutes (pro tip: we use circular cast-iron souffle bowls), or cook in a pan.
• You can also make omelets by pouring a thin coat on a non-stick ban, cooking on one side until the chickpea scramble sticks together, then carefully flip and add cheeze and other fixin's.

PAIRING SUGGESTIONS

Brunch post hardcore paddle-board session.

La Tortuga

And what of the 1988 Aerostar touring van, one might ask. It was conventionally a vehicle, sure, in that it cut a cool swath of quicksilver across the highways and bi-ways of North America. Seen from space, it was bliss. But the Aerostar touring van was also a rockstar dressing room-SLASH-sleeping bunk-SLASH-vegan food laboratory (when retro-fitted with a hotplate plugged into the cigarette lighter). The scent was a conflation of slow-roasted jackfruit carnitas, multi-use coconut oil, and rock-and-roll. Randy referred to the Aerostar as "Speed Dog's Ashram," as he had besmirched upon it a superabundance of righteous energy.

"So long as it can be a non-denominational ashram," quipped Speed Dog, not hip to the religious gravy.

Rach, Aunt Louise's marketing manager at the *Lake Erie Weekly Herald*, was on the road with the pair, for research for Jean-Claude van Randy and Speed Dog's new column in the *Herald*, and also for something that might spice up her everyday routine. She was starting to feel boxed in by the Cleveland, Geneva-on-the-Lake, and Upper Ashtabula triangle and craved some adventure. Her marketing mentor in New York had referred to her fully rational life-transition home as "crawling back into the womb of the Midwest."

Rach chuckled atop the lip of her chipotle-infused mezcal cocktail she couldn't afford at the honky-tonk-themed bar and cat café in Brooklyn when her mentor suggested as much, but as a millennial she possessed opinions. Many opinions. Also: ideas. Big ideas. And if realistic financial decisions forced her to pool her resources while she established her career in marketing and began paying off her student loans and modest credit card debt, then she was determined to make the best of her situation. New York was for rich kids and Russians, and Rach was neither.

Rach, Randy, and Speed Dog had just descended from the Sangre de Cristo Mountains and were parked near a spring outside of Alamosa, where they planned to bunk for the night. That day, a hair before noon, they had summited Blanca Peak. Speed Dog, at the fore of the group, let out a wild mountain yawp. Surveying the panorama, Rach was awe-struck. The Hudson, the East River, nor Lake Erie held a vegan candle to this.

As a fire whipped within the ring at their campsite, Randy and Speed Dog huddled between the hot plate, a sixer of local craft beer, and a well-traveled bamboo cutting board.

Groggy from the summit, Rach reposed upon the streambed, sweaty beer in hand, toes in the cool mountain water. Speed Dog's yawp was a blistering shriek across the void, but Rach felt this same aliveness, this same superabundance of wild energy now. She thought about her mentor, a publicist drunk on hyperbole, and how she had made the right decision in moving to the Midwest to work in marketing with Louise at the newspaper. She thought about how one day she would one-up the Drunk Publicist. In her imagined scenario, this would be in a public setting, brimming with social media tastemakers. (It's not vindictive when you're right.)

Randy let out a call for supper, and Rach joined the guys. She was still enjoying her fantasies of one-upping her ex-mentor as she dug into the meal. It was sudden, like a thunderclap from Heaven if Heaven existed (it might, maybe — no one knows). The flavor, the texture, the sensation: it was like the summit of Blanca Peak: there was truth and wild energy to life, and maybe this was it.

"You guys, what the fuck is this?" Rach asked.

"Dinner," said Speed Dog.

"Dinner?"

Randy cleared his throat. "This is a Turtle, topped with a chili-lime slaw and simple remoulade."

"The fuck's a Turtle?" Rach asked.

Speed Dog shrugged.

"We make 'em a lot on the road," said Randy. "We cook a bunch of stuff — this evening we made a vegan buffalo macaroni and cheeze with gluten-free rotini, seasoned taco 'beef,' sautéed vegetables, and pickled jalapeños — and then stuffed it inside a giant burrito tortilla, and then baked it in the solar-powered convection oven till it's got a nice crispy shell. Don't know why we used gluten-free rotini in a gluten-full tortilla, but sometimes you don't ask questions when you're hungry."

"And that's how it got its name: cause it looks like a cute little turtle," Speed Dog said.

TORTUGA

"You're a rockstar," Rach said in disbelief, an accusative finger leveled at Speed Dog. "And you're a Jean-Claude, for goodness sake," Rach said, in further disbelief, turning her accusative finger to Randy. "You're using the wrong adjectives!"

She saw in this something-like-a-baked-burrito her opportunity, her ticket to one-up her ex-mentor, the Drunk Publicist. Ideally publicly and in front of a gaggle of social media tastemakers.

Rach slammed her craft beer upon the picnic table. "Where's your sense of drama? A 'turtle' is a sundae. This isn't a turtle; this is really, really good sex in tortilla form. You need a better name."

"I kinda like 'Turtle,'" said Speed Dog.

Rach shot him a look and he quickly apologized.

"Looks like we've got a mystery on our hands," Randy said. "A name mystery."

Rach smirked. "No, it's not a mystery. And we're not eating a 'Turtle.'" She picked her sunglasses up from the picnic table and put them on, smirking further. "This, this is a Tortuga."

"Isn't that just Spanish for *turtle*?" Randy asked.

Rach shot him a look and he quickly apologized. ∎

Pambazo — p. 64

LUNCH & SAMMIES

Great Sausage Sammy
Sausage, pickles, pickled onions, tomato,
cheeze, and chimichurri.

GREAT SAUSAGE SAMMY

THE DISH: This thick-sliced sausage sandwich is hearty, and, combined with chimichurri, packs a punch of flavor. Vegan hunger demons, beware!

SAUSAGE RECIPE

1 cup beans
1 tablespoon chili powder
1 tablespoon fennel (or anise)
2 tablespoons brown sugar
1 tablespoon smoked paprika
1 tablespoon oregano
2 teaspoons crushed red pepper
2 tablespoons nutritional yeast
1 teaspoon pepper
2 tablespoons maple syrup
1 tablespoon barbecue sauce
1 teaspoon garlic powder
1½ cups vegetable broth
1 teaspoon liquid smoke
2½ cups vital wheat gluten

CHEFFING INSTRUCTIONS

- Add all ingredients except wheat gluten to blend and mix thoroughly.
- Add wheat gluten to mixing bowl and pour in spice blend. Stir mixture and then knead with hands.
- Form the mixture into logs, wrap in aluminum foil, and steam over boiling water for an hour.
- You can then slice the logs length-wise or into circular pieces.
- Store in marinade and simply heat to serve.

ASSEMBLY

We put pickles, sausage, scallion cheddar cheeze spread, pickled onions, tomato, chimichurri, and sometimes slaw on this sammy.

PAMBAZO

THE DISH: This Mexico City-style "wet" sandwich will have you dousing everything in hot sauce. It's a little sloppy when you're getting a face-full of hot sauce, so refrain from eating this on first dates. Or second dates.

WALNUT CHORIZO RECIPE

1 cup walnuts

1½ cups black beans

¼ cup oil

2 tablespoons apple cider vinegar

¼ onion, diced

3 pieces garlic, diced

2 tablespoons oregano

1 teaspoon crushed red pepper

2 teaspoons brown sugar

3 teaspoons cinnamon

2 tablespoons chili powder

4 tablespoons crushed tomato

CHEFFING INSTRUCTIONS

• Add walnuts, black beans, oil, and vinegar to blend. Pulse in blender, but don't pulverize.

• Dice garlic and onion and sauté with light oil in a pan.

• Combine contents from blender with onions/garlic in a mixing bowl and add spices, stirring together sufficiently.

• In 400° oven, put mixture in a pan and bake until chorizo begins to dry.

ASSEMBLY

• Pour hot sauce of choice on a dish and dip the outside of the sandwich bun until coated and then heat bun on low-heat in pan until toasted.

• Add: slaw, salsa, buffalo queso, aioli, fresh cilantro, ed potatoes.

PAIRING SUGGESTIONS

Mariachi music, and a cool breeze after a long day's work.

Pambazo
Walnut chorizo with potatoes, slaw, buffalo queso, salsa,
fresh cilantro, and aioli, on a bun dipped in hot sauce and baked.

Eggplant Po' Boy
Cajun eggplant, slaw, lettuce, tomato, and remoulade.

SECOND PAIR OF BLACK JEANS EGGPLANT PO' BOY

THE DISH: Look, the primary format we choose to slay Vegan Hunger Demons is sandwich form, and this is one of our all-time favorites, a solid A+ drum solo if ever there was one.

BREADED CAJUN EGGPLANT RECIPE

~¼ cup plant-based milk
zest of 1 lemon
2 teaspoons salt
1 cup cornmeal

1 eggplant, skin on, sliced ¼" thick
1½ cups flour
1 tablespoon cajun spice
3 tablespoons lemon juice

CHEFFING INSTRUCTIONS

- In a mixing bowl, add flour, lemon juice + zest, spices, and milk, and stir until it resembles a thick pancake batter.
- Dip eggplant slices in batter and then coat in cornmeal.
- Fry eggplant in oil in a pan.

ASSEMBLY

Add some slaw, lettuce, tomato, and a zesty remoulade to this eggplant for a classic New Orleans-style Po' Boy sandwich.

PAIRING SUGGESTIONS

Wendell Pierce.

BACKYARD VEGGIE BURGER

THE DISH: You can find veggie burgers in any frozen foods section, and many of them are delightful. However, you're going to need a hearty house-made patty if you're going to impress your step-dad. This veggie burger recipe will make Keith's eyebrows arch behind his Foakleys.

BURGER PATTY RECIPE

1 cup walnuts
1 cup pinto beans
1 tablespoon oregano
2 tablespoons tomato paste
1 tablespoon ranch dressing
1 tablespoon barbecue sauce
1 teaspoon mustard

2 teaspoons onion powder
1 teaspoon salt + pepper + sugar
3 pieces garlic
1 teaspoon smoked paprika
1 teaspoon liquid smoke
1 cup quinoa
1 cup vital wheat gluten

CHEFFING INSTRUCTIONS

- Add everything except wheat gluten and quinoa to blender and pulverize.
- In mixing bowl, add wheat gluten, quinoa, and blender contents and stir thoroughly. Add additional wheat gluten by the tablespoon until the mixture is hearty.
- Form the mixture into patties on a pan. You can either bake, pan-fry, or the patties. Sprinkle some onion powder, salt, and pepper on top of the patties.

PAIRING SUGGESTIONS

Sweaty beer in a go-to koozie while coaching the charcoal like a boss.

Backyard Burger

Fishless Filet
Fishless filet with buffalo queso on the left, and a more traditional fishless filet with tartar sauce on the right. Both scrumptious.

FISHLESS FILET

THE DISH: These fishless filets don't have to be on burger buns, but can also make for fish & chips or other boardwalk favorites.

TARTAR SAUCE RECIPE

3 cups oil

¼ cup diced pickles

¼ cup diced red onion

zest of 1 lemon

1 cup aquafaba

3 tablespoons lemon juice

1 teaspoon sugar + salt + pepper

~1¼ cups tapioca powder

TARTAR SAUCE CHEFFING INSTRUCTIONS

• Add aquafaba, lemon juice, sugar, salt, pepper, tapioca flour, and oil to blender and blend thoroughly until resembles creamy mayonnaise.

• Add diced pickles, onion, and lemon zest to blender slowly until mixed.

Kentucky Waterfall

EGGPLANT CHEFFING INSTRUCTIONS

• Peel eggplant skin, and slice into ½" pieces.

• Prepare the batter the same way you do for fishless tacos (p. 35) and fry eggplant in oil.

ASSEMBLY

Add filets to buns with lettuce and tartar sauce. Enjoy.

PAIRING SUGGESTIONS

Boardwalks. Damp beach towels. Sand lingering between your toes.

Second Pair of Black Jeans Eggplant Po' Boy

Where the Delaware Bay converges with the Atlantic Ocean at the Cape May Peninsula, Randy, Speed Dog, and Rach sat on an electric golf cart that Aunt Louise's friend, Doris, let them borrow. The Aerostar touring van was in repose for the day in Doris's carport beside her purple Victorian manse near Cape May's downtown corridor.

Doris was a confidante of Speed Dog's Aunt Louise, dating back to her Gordon Lightfoot days, and had recently come into financial distress. Since she had settled in Cape May in the late 1970s, the town had become a popular vacation hub, sending real estate prices skyrocketing (she blamed the Rich and the Russians for absconding down the coast from New York City). Doris owned a community garden near the Washington Street Mall, where developers plotted devilishly to erect a four-story condominium complex modeled after an original four-story condo complex a block away.

"Just what the world needs," Speed Dog sighed. "More beige condos, more cargo shorts, more frozen food."

Randy glanced to the horizon, chin crooked upon his fist. "Looks like we've got another mystery on our hands."

It had been Rach's idea to volunteer Randy and Speed Dog to Doris. Their column in the *Lake Erie Weekly Herald* was now syndicated in fifty-eight papers coast-to-coast, and the week before, Moby had tweeted about them. Natalie Portman sent them a postcard from her movie set on the Ambergris Caye in Belize.

"All you guys gotta do," Rach had said, enthusiastically pacing in her black jeans and black faux-leather jacket with black t-shirt, "is bring some of your newly acquired prestige to Doris's cause, stage an event that doubles as a fundraiser, and then write about it. In the process, we'll bring Doris out of the red and into the green."

An instant later, Randy'd chuckled. "I get what you did there, and I like it."

Rach had shot him a glance, and he'd ceased.

After Denny had unsuccessfully proposed a vegan ranch dressing contest (the guy was simply insatiable when it came to ranch dressing), he'd done some digging and discovered that New Jersey grows the bulk of the United States' eggplants. Rach had suggested an eggplant cook-off, with Randy and Speed Dog competing.

The cook-off was that night, and Rach was more nervous than both Randy and Speed Dog combined, owing to the fact that she spotted her ex-mentor, the Drunk Publicist, sipping a bellini on the patio of Loki's Saloon on the Washington Street Mall while Rach was out for her morning jog. Could it be a coincidence? Hahaha, JK, LOL, no way! The Drunk Publicist was up to her deviant ways, and Rach knew it. She had to change into a second pair of black jeans — her lucky pair — she was so nervous.

As the time for the eggplant cook-off approached, a crowd assembled at the mall which now had a bandstand sans band at the forefront. The Drunk Publicist was perched in the same exact position on a stool on Loki's patio, her arm crooked to support her bellini, observing the festivities. Rach watched; she couldn't tell if they made eye contact because the Drunk Publicist's eyes were concealed behind oversized gradient sunglasses. Rach knew something diabolical was afoot.

Doris — in her role as emcee and part of the 3-person eggplant cook-off jury — took the microphone, cut a ribbon, and introduced the festivities by riffing on a classic Gordon Lightfoot diddy so the crowd was absolutely boot-stomping.

There were seven participants in the eggplant cook-off, including Randy and Speed Dog, and the dishes ranged from eggplant parmigiana, to a classic eggplant Bolognese, to an eggplant rollatini, to a vegan eggplant saltimbocca, to even an eggplant "meat"ball sub with peppers and onions (it was Jersey, after all, so *fuggedaboudit*).

EGGPLANT

Randy crafted his riff on a po' boy, subbing in Cajun corn-meal-crusted eggplant, while Speed Dog opted to go with his Aunt Louise-inspired Not Even Lake Erie Perch Fishless Tacos.

Doris and the jury were stumped, in a good way. While they were grateful for Randy and Speed Dog sharing the vegan spotlight, they also desired for someone from the community to win the $20 gift certificate to Pizza on the Port and the free round of mini-golf. Also: glory.

While the jury was deliberating, a white guy with dreads in attendance was stoking tensions, and not in a wholesome way. "This is bogus," he called out to the crowd. "Veggies are for sides, not a main dish."

A few in the crowd snickered, and a handful of bystanders in the back shuffled away from the eggplant cook-off in agreement.

"I got ya eggplant right here," the white guy with dreads called out. Not wholesome at all. This spurred a gaggle of middle-aged folks in visors to skedaddle to their electric golf cart and putter away.

The Drunk Publicist

Randy and Speed Dog exchanged side-eyes. Rach was on the balls of her feet. She looked to her ex-mentor, the Drunk Publicist, who was frozen on the patio at Loki's, bellini crooked aloft as if extending a cheers; this was her doing, and Rach knew it.

"Where you even supposed to get your protein?" The white guy with dreads' voice was rising, and a small circle had opened up around him. "Without protein you won't be able to go to the beach, play shuffle-board, lift your grand-kids off the ground, or work a full day. Veganism is for the radicalized far-left."

A few in the crowd went so far as to clap; for some it was a triggered auto-reply to the phrase "radicalized far-left," arriving without actual thought on their behalf.

Doris was concerned; the jury had halted their deliberations. The white guy with dreads was derailing the entire eggplant cook-off, and the fundraiser looked like it was about to end in catastrophe.

Doris's community garden would be transformed into yet another beige condominium complex.

Rach, cheeks in palms, looked to the Drunk Publicist, whose stoicism was victory enough. Rach then turned to Randy and Speed Dog in exasperation.

Jean-Claude van Randy and Speed Dog had had enough. "There are a number of flaws in this interloper's argument," Randy called out as they descended from the bandstand stairs and made their way through the crowd to the white guy with dreads. "The first, and most glaring dissension from fact is that vegetables do have protein. A peanut butter and jelly sandwich is a complete protein, and oftentimes is greater in protein than a greasy burger. So let's put that argument to bed."

While Randy sidled up to the white guy with dreads, Speed Dog meandered through the crowd to the Drunk Publicist.

"The second," Randy chuckled, "is that this white guy with dreads is not actually a white guy with dreads."

Randy looked to Speed Dog standing beside the Drunk Publicist, and nodded. Speed Dog faced the Drunk Publicist on the patio of Loki's Saloon, extended his pinkie finger, and nudged her over, causing her to crash to the ground. Or, rather, a cardboard cut-out of her.

A number of the crowd gasped in horror.

At this exact moment, Randy tugged on the hair of the white guy with dreads, removing the dreads completely from his head in a fistfull, to reveal that the dreads were in fact a wig. And this wig was a disguise worn by none other than the Drunk Publicist!

The Drunk Publicist shuffled back and forth, head on pivot. "All I'm saying is, eggplant sucks. Why not veal? Community gardens are for the birds. Am I right?"

The Drunk Publicist looked to the crowd for agreement, but they all shook their heads in disappointment and disgust, and removed their checkbooks from their striped-shorts pockets to cut a check for Doris's community garden.

"How did you know?" Rach asked the guys.

"Loki is the trickster god," Randy said.

"And she sat on that patio for seven hours without moving or sipping her bellini," Speed Dog added.

"I'd have gotten away with it, too, if it weren't for those meddling vegans!" the Drunk Publicist called out as she was led away by the Cape May Neighborhood Watch. ■

LARGE PLATES

Mexxxy Enchiladas — p. 83

Mexxxy Enchiladas
Toss rice or quinoa with chick'n or seasoned "beef," roasted poblano peppers, cheeze, and jalapeños, then layer in tortillas and top with enchilada sauce, stripe with aioli, and splash on some slaw

MEXXXY ENCHILADAS

THE DISH: Don't bother rolling the toppings in the tortillas; we layer our enchiladas like lasagna, keeping it messy and deconstructed.

ROASTED GARLIC ENCHILADA SAUCE RECIPE

½ teaspoon cumin
1 teaspoon cinnamon
1 teaspoon salt
1 teaspoon sugar
6 cups vegetable broth
2 teaspoons crushed red pepper
1 tablespoon apple cider vinegar

¼ cup oil
¼ cup flour
6 tablespoon chili powder
12 tablespoons crushed tomatoes
8 pieces garlic, roasted in oven until blackened

Enchilada

CHEFFING INSTRUCTIONS

• Heat oil in pan, then add flour.
• In blender, combine spices, garlic, crushed tomatoes, and 1 cup vegetable broth.
• Add blender contents to pan and stir.
• Add remaining vegetable broth one cup at a time to sauce, stirring constantly, while gradually reducing heat. Once all the vegetable broth has been added to the sauce, reduce heat and allow to simmer on low heat for an hour.
• Toss seasoned rice with chick'n, roasted poblano peppers, smoky mozzarella cheeze, and vegetables, then layer with tortillas and smother with enchilada sauce.

CLASSY ITALIAN CASSEROLE

THE DISH: Hearty Italian food is good year round. Once you master a few basics, like a simple marinara sauce and ricotta cheeze, you'll have the main components to do stuffed shells, manicotti, lasagna, and eggplant or chick'n parmigiana.

RICOTTA CHEEZE RECIPE

2 cups cashews
1 cup water
¼ cup nutritional yeast
1 tablespoon apple cider vinegar
3 tablespoons lemon juice
2 tablespoons hummus (see simple recipe p. 116)
Salt + pepper to taste

CHEEZE IS THE BEST!

CHEFFING INSTRUCTIONS

- Fry eggplant and cook noodles.
- Make a classy Italian sauce by sautéing onions, peppers, garlic, and spices with crushed tomatoes and oil.
- In a pan, layer noodles with ricotta cheeze and fried eggplant, before topping with generous amount of tomato sauce.
- Garnish with shredded cheeze and fresh oregano.

PAIRING SUGGESTIONS

Red table wine with a classy napkin tied around it that you insist on pouring for guests.
Italian brothers-in-law.

Classy Italian Casserole

Leigh's Late-Night Trip to Taco Town
Chick'n wangs tossed in barbecue sauce with slaw,
salsa, coconut bacon, cheeze, and farmhouse ranch dressing.

LEIGH'S LATE-NIGHT TRIP TO TACO TOWN

THE DISH: These barbecue chick'n tacos call on some previous recipes in this *Guide to Vegan Cooking*, including the game-day chick'n wangs (p. 25), coconut bacon (p. 50), salsa (p. 115), smoky mozzarella cheeze (p. 19), and barbecue sauce.

RANCH DRESSING RECIPE

1 tablespoon apple cider vinegar
5–7 pieces of garlic
2 teaspoons dill
2 teaspoons onion powder

1 cup aquafaba
3 tablespoons lemon juice
1 teaspoon sugar + salt + pepper
~1¼ cups tapioca flour
3 cups oil

CHEFFING INSTRUCTIONS

• Add aquafaba, lemon juice, sugar, salt, pepper, tapioca flour, and oil to blender and pulverize until it resembles creamy mayo.
• Add garlic, vinegar, dill, onion powder, and continue to blend.

ASSEMBLY

Warm corn tortillas. Fry chick'n wangs before tossing with barbecue sauce. Add the wangs to tortillas, then top with slaw, salsa, coconut bacon, shredded cheeze, and farmhouse ranch dressing.

SPECIAL BONUS STREET SAUCE RECIPE

We use ranch to make our "street sauce," a riff on a fast food chain's signature sauce: 1 cup ranch, ½ cup mustard, and ½ cup barbecue sauce. Tastes like honey mustard.

Chile Relleno
Roasted poblano pepper, stuffed with goodness,
topped with roasted garlic enchilada sauce.

CHILE RELLENO

THE DISH: Chile rellenos, done well, will make your tastebuds do a happy dance. You will need time and patience, as they do require some dexterity.

CHILE RELLENO RECIPE

1 cup grated cheeze (see p. 19)
1 cup seasoned rice
1 cup seasoned flour for breading

6 poblano peppers
1 cup seasoned "beef"
(see recipe on p. 32)

CHEFFING INSTRUCTIONS

- Heat poblano peppers in oven at 350° until they begin to blacken.
- After allowing poblanos to cool, peel skin from outside. Slice peppers length-wise and remove seeds from inside.
- Combine "beef," cheeze, and rice, and stuff inside poblanos.
- In a bowl, mix flour with seasoning and plant-based milk to form batter.
- Heat oil in pan, carefully dip stuffed poblanos in batter and fry, seam-side down. Carefully flip poblanos and fry top-side.

ASSEMBLY

Place fried poblano peppers on a bed of seasoned rice, smother with roasted garlic enchilada sauce (see recipe on p. 83), and top with fresh cilantro, pickled onions, aioli, and more grated cheeze.

PAIRING SUGGESTIONS

Anyone you want to impress with your cheffing prowess.
Instead of "beef," include hearts of palm to make a "Seafood" Relleno.

The Morning After Randy Saw The Flaming Lips at the Henry Miller Memorial Library, Big Sur, California

In the land of cheese, chairs, and churches (Sheboygan), what's a non-denominational, plant-based Jean-Claude to do? Spread your wings, that's what. Spread your wings and fly away.

Big Sur, California, was Speed Dog's third favorite place with "Big" in its name (following Big Sky Country [1.] and the Big Idaho Potato [2.] [the latter strictly for sentimental memories of a romantic weekend tryst with a Minnesotan sweetheart who went by the name Luanne]). Randy and Speed Dog had been invited to a special performance at the Henry Miller Memorial Library in Big Sur, by none other than The Flaming Lips, who were admirers of their syndicated vegan food column in the *Lake Erie Weekly Herald*, and pals with Moby, who was an even bigger admirer and would be at the show. Rach was palling along, keeping Randy and Speed Dog on task, and managing the crew's social media accounts.

Randy was in the backseat, finding inner balance, when Speed Dog ushered the Aerostar to the berm of a crowded scenic vista. There, Randy found himself surrounded by what he would later describe to bar-hands coast-to-coast as "beatniks; you know, long-hairs."

The Flaming Lips were in Big Sur, and wouldn't you know it!

Speed Dog, having once served as roadie for the Lips, recognized some of the fans, who pulled him and Rach along to the show. Randy needed some "me time," so he yanked his climbing harness and gloves from the Aerostar, and descended the cliff-side to a narrow swath of sand where he meditated and did yoga as the sun set and stars began to dimple the ocean-scape.

At the Henry Miller Memorial Library, the crowd was clumped in various social pockets around the grounds, waiting for the Lips to take the stage. While Speed Dog cavorted with familiar faces, Rach sipped an overpriced craft beer.

"*OMG*, Rach, is that you?" a voice called out.

Rach turned around to see none other than her nemesis, her ex-mentor, the Drunk Publicist, whose oversized gradient sunglasses swallowed her face. A chill ran down Rach's spine. "What are you doing in Big Sur?" Rach asked, as cool and nonchalant as she could muster.

"Oh, sweetie, this is like the Coachella of subversive indie culture — The Flaming Lips at the memorial of the inspiration for the Beat Generation. Totes heavy; totes *my scene*. As soon as I heard about it, I knew I just *had* to be here."

Rach immediately realized that something was awry. Ever since the Drunk Publicist's humiliating public uncovering of her white guy with dreads disguise in Cape May at Doris's first annual eggplant cook-off, Rach understood that she'd be back, and more hyperbolic than ever.

The opening band's set ended with a dramatic, life-affirming crescendo, and Speed Dog let out a mighty yawp. Having found inner balance, Randy had joined Rach, who pointed out the Drunk Publicist. She was now behind a vendor's stand, speaking across the booth to a number of excitable social media influencers, hawking a knockoff Ring Pop product called "Jinkies."

"Jinkies," Randy said, reading the name. "Is that a breakfast cereal or something?"

Jinkies were like Ring Pops, but also not: they were bracelets with a candy ring on top. And the Drunk Publicist, realizing that The Flaming Lips were a bunch of animal-loving rockstars, was marketing Jinkies as vegan.

Rach and Randy approached the Jinkies booth. A gaggle of social media influencers were simultaneously looking fabulous AF and scrolling through their feeds or captioning a caption.

"Oh, I'm glad you're here," the Drunk Publicist called out to Randy. She turned to the social media influencers. "As you may know, Jean-Claude van Randy is a celebrity vegan food columnist for the *Lake Erie Weekly Herald*." The Drunk Publicist swiveled to Randy. "Would you like to try a Jinkies, Randall?"

"I'd love to," Randy said.

Rach curled into Randy's shoulder. "What are you doing?" Rach whisper-shouted. "You're falling into her trap."

The Drunk Publicist handed Randy a Jinkies candy bracelet Ring Pop knockoff across the booth while the social media influencers got their camera-phones into position to snap a pic for their feed.

The Jinkies looked like bliss in candy bracelet form, and shimmered beneath The Flaming Lips light show like some mystical totem.

"This looks spectacular," Randy said. "But before I dig in, I always double-check my ingredients list."

"Jinkies are the best 100% vegan candy product on the market," the Drunk Publicist proclaimed hyperbolically, extending a wrapper to Randy. "They're like if you crossed a fire emoji with a free-spirited female surfer emoji; they're *that* good."

Randy squinted his eyes, perusing the list. "Looks like we've got another mystery on our hands," he said.

"A mystery?" the Drunk Publicist asked. "Aren't they just simply *that* good?"

"Good enough for Christian rock," Randy quipped.

"And why is that, pray tell?" A bead of sweat had formed along the Drunk Publicist's upper lip and Rach spotted it. The social media influencers had to sense it; the scene was electric.

Randy returned the Jinkies label to the Drunk Publicist. "Castoreum."

"Castor oil? What's that."

"That's beaver ▪ juice," one social media influencer quipped, hip to the vegan gravy.

"Well, not exactly beaver ▪ juice," Randy explained, "but rather, castoreum comes from glands that resemble testicles directly adjacent to the beaver's ▪."

The line of social media influencers gasped. The Drunk Publicist gasped. The Flaming Lips — having taken Speed Dog on stage with them for a solid A+ drum solo — were between songs, and gasped.

"Surely that can't be," the Drunk Publicist exclaimed. "It must be a misprint."

Meanwhile, the silent camera-phone shutters of the dozens of social media influencers snapped away unabashedly at the spectacle, while Rach observed, satisfied.

The Jinkies stand was shut down by security, for the Jinkies staff's own safety. Speed Dog closed out the Lips' set on a triumphant note and was carried off stage on the shoulders of adoring fans. Big Sur was truly blissed out.

The next morning, a sleepless Speed Dog followed the Aerostar's GPS directions to a plant-based watering hole, where Randy ordered not one, but two breakfast burritos. It was decadence, central California-style, and he'd remember it for the rest of his days. ▪

MUNCHIES

Beer Brats — p. 103

TACO MAC & CHEEZE TORTUGA

THE DISH: These taco mac & cheeze Tortugas will make you believe in immortality. Beware, it's all you'll eat for the next month.

ASSEMBLY

- Toss cooked noodles in buffalo queso (p. 13), add seasoned "beef" (p. 32), jalapeños, diced tomatoes, shredded smoky mozzarella cheeze (p. 19), and warm on low heat.
- On a large quesadilla-sized tortilla, add more shredded cheeze to the center. Add the warmed taco mac & cheeze to the tortilla, and fold in the corners to seal closed the proper Tortuga pocket.
- To make a proper Tortuga, you'll want to bake it, seam down, on a pan in the oven, so that the tortilla becomes crispy. (If, say, you're starving or stoned or drunk, you can heat the Tortuga in a sprayed pan.)

PAIRING SUGGESTIONS

Following a long hike through the woods.
Lukewarm lagers around a campfire.

Taco Mac & Cheeze Tortuga

Gobbler Tortuga
Turkey, smashed potatoes, and cranberry sauce
stuffed in a tortilla and baked until crispy.
Topped with mushroom gravy.

GOBBLER TORTUGA

THE DISH: Tortugas 4-eva. This Tortuga has all the holiday fixin's stuffed in a flour tortilla, which is then baked and topped with gravy.

TURKEY RECIPE

1 teaspoon onion powder
5 cloves garlic
2 teaspoons pepper
1½ cups gravy mix
2½ cups vital wheat gluten

1 cup cooked potato
½ cup beans*
4 tablespoons nutritional yeast
2 tablespoons "poultry seasoning"
1 teaspoon sage

CHEFFING INSTRUCTIONS

- In a blender, add cooked potato, beans and spices.
- Add wheat gluten to a mixing bowl, and add blender contents.
- Stir the dough and knead until desired consistency is achieved.
- Shape the turkey dough into six sausage-shaped logs.
- Steam logs over high water for at least a half-hour on each side.

ASSEMBLY

- Slice turkey and add, with cranberry sauce and mashed potatoes, to a flour tortilla, and bake.
- Once tortilla is firm, top with preferred gravy.

PAIRING SUGGESTIONS

Sweaters, a fire in the hearth, hot toddies, or spiked egg nog.

*great northern or garbanzos work best

NACHO MAMA'S HOME FRIES

THE DISH: Look, you gotta do some kind of nachos. You need it for the big game or John Candy movie night, or even if you're hungry and feeling feisty. Rather than a plateful of chips, we recommend using home fries for an even heartier base.

ASSEMBLY
- Make a mountain of home fries on a plate.
- Top home fries with everything in your fridge (i.e. buffalo queso, shredded smoky mozzarella cheeze, slaw, salsa, pickled onions, guacamole, sour cream).
- Stripe with colorful aioli.
- Garnish with fresh cilantro.

BEER BRATS

THE DISH: This recipe for beer brats is really just a few slight tweaks — such as mustard and beer — to our original sausage recipe.

SAUSAGE RECIPE

1 cup beans	2 tablespoons nutritional yeast
1 tablespoon chili powder	1 teaspoon pepper
1 tablespoon fennel (or anise)	2 tablespoons mustard
2 tablespoons brown sugar	1 cup beer
1 tablespoon smoked paprika	1 teaspoon garlic powder
1 tablespoon oregano	½ cup vegetable broth
2 teaspoons crushed red pepper	1 teaspoon liquid smoke
	2½ cups vital wheat gluten

CHEFFING INSTRUCTIONS

- Add all ingredients except wheat gluten and mix thoroughly.
- Add wheat gluten to mixing bowl and pour in spice blend. Stir mixture and then knead with hands.
- Form mixture into brat-shaped logs, wrap in aluminum foil, and steam over a mixture of boiling water, beer, garlic for an hour.
- Unwrap brats, which you can then heat on a or pan with oil.

PAIRING SUGGESTIONS

We've topped these beer brats with a classic sauerkraut and mustard combo, as well as made Coneys by topping with chili and grated cheddar cheeze, but our personal favorite is to top these with sautéed cabbage, pickles, and street sauce.

Scandalous Tacos

SCANDALOUS TACOS

THE DISH: Tacos with the hot sauce baked into the tortilla.
What else ya want?

SMOKY DOJO HOT SAUCE RECIPE

2 habaneros

3 jalapeños

3 pieces garlic

2 tablespoons smoked paprika

2 teaspoons celery salt

1 cup water

½ cup white vinegar

1 teaspoon sugar

¼ teaspoon xanthan gum (in a separate bowl,
combine with 2 tablespoons water, stir, and let sit)

TASTY AF

CHEFFING INSTRUCTIONS

• Roast habaneros and jalapeños in oven in low heat until
the peppers' skin begins to blacken.

• Add all ingredients except xanthan gum to blender and pulverize.

• Once mixture is sufficiently blended, add xanthan gum and
pulverize for an additional minute so that the hot sauce
has a less liquidy consistency.

ASSEMBLY

Coat one side of tortilla with hot sauce and bake until tortilla begins
to absorb sauce. Then place tortilla dry side down and layer in taco
ingredients of your choosing. Devour.

Maple-Frosted Cookie Dough Bars — p. 110

Devilish Cheezecake

DEVILISH CHEEZECAKE (GLUTEN-FREE)

THE DISH: We're bonkers about cheeze (obvs), so when we go sweet we go cheezy with a cheezecake. You can top this with a fruit glaze, or just hammer away with it as is. This vegan cheezecake is not raw, but baked.

CRUST RECIPE

1¼ cups gluten-free oats
1¼ cups almonds
¼ cup vegan butter
4 tablespoons sugar
7 tablespoon coconut oil

CHEEZECAKE FILLING RECIPE

1¼ cups raw, unsalted cashews
1⅔ cup coconut cream
1 8-ounce block tofu
2 teaspoons vanilla extract
1 cup sugar
2 tablespoons coconut oil
zest of 1 lemon
4 tablespoons lemon juice
2 tablespoons corn starch
1 tablespoon maple syrup

CHEFFING INSTRUCTIONS

- Blend crust ingredients and add to 8x10 baking pan.
- Bake crust at 350° for 10 minutes.
- After soaking cashews in warm water, add all filling ingredients to blender and pulverize. Pour filling on top of crust in baking pan.
- Bake cheezecake at 350° for 40 minutes, until golden on top.

PAIRING SUGGESTIONS

This cheezecake is rich, but not overly heavy.
Dust with powdered sugar and candied fruit.

MAPLE-FROSTED COOKIE DOUGH BARS (GLUTEN-FREE)

THE DISH: These cookie dough bars are delightful, but not overly decadent, while the chickpeas provide a nice chewiness. The maple frosting gives it that jolt of sweetness that puts it over the top.

COOKIE DOUGH BAR RECIPE

4 cups chickpeas
¾ cup plant-based milk
½ tablespoon vinegar
½ cup vegan butter
3 teaspoons vanilla
1¼ cups sugar
1¼ cups almond flour
1 teaspoon baking powder
½ teaspoon salt
1 cup chocolate chips

MAPLE FROSTING RECIPE

1 cup vegan butter
3 tablespoons maple syrup
1 tablespoon plant-based milk
2 cups powdered sugar

CHEFFING INSTRUCTIONS

- Add chickpeas, milk, vinegar, butter, and vanilla to a blender and mix.
- In mixing bowl, combine sugar, almond flour, baking powder, salt, and chocolate chips. Pour wet ingredients into mixing bowl and stir.
- Bake cookie dough bars at 350° for 30 minutes, or until golden brown on top and the center is no longer jiggly.
- Add frosting ingredients to bowl and mix with hand mixer.
- Allow cookie dough bars to cool for 10 minutes, then without a cover in fridge for an hour before topping with frosting.

Maple-Frosted Cookie Dough Bars

VEGAN LIFE-HACKS

Mayonnaise (or Aioli, if you're fancy) — p. 114

MAYONNAISE (OR AIOLI, IF YOU'RE FANCY)

THE DISH: Figuring out how to make our own mayonnaise from scratch using aquafaba was a life-saver. Vegan mayo is pretty pricey at stores, and we use this creamy mayo as a base for everything from our farmhouse ranch dressing, to tartar sauce, remoulade, and on and on.

INGREDIENTS

1 cup aquafaba

3 tablespoons lemon juice

1 teaspoon sugar + salt + pepper

~1¼ cups tapioca flour

3 cups oil

1 tablespoon apple cider vinegar

5–7 pieces garlic

2 teaspoons dill

2 teaspoons onion powder

CHEFFING INSTRUCTIONS

- Add aquafaba, lemon juice, sugar, salt, pepper, tapioca flour, and oil to a blender and pulverize until resembles a creamy mayonnaise. Add additional tapioca flour or aquafaba until achieves desired consistency.

PAIRING SUGGESTIONS

Mix with sriracha for sriracha aioli. Add something like roasted red peppers to impress bougie friends. The only thing holding you back is your imagination.

SALSA

THE DISH: If we had to compare this salsa to a baseball bullpen, this would be the ace bullpen of the 1990 World Series Champion Cincinnati Reds, because it's Nasty Boys! (In a good way.)

SALSA RECIPE

5–7 roma tomatoes
1½ cups crushed tomatoes
2 teaspoons salt
1½ teaspoons sugar
1 fresh jalapeño, seeded and diced
3 tablespoons lime juice
¼ red onion, diced
½ cup fresh cilantro, diced

CHEFFING INSTRUCTIONS

• Add fresh tomatoes and crushed tomatoes to blender and mix.
• Add remainder of ingredients and pulse, but don't pulverize.

PAIRING SUGGESTIONS

This is a great game-day dip.
You can also throw it on tacos, burritos, or sandwiches.

HUMMUS

THE DISH: You need a go-to hummus recipe handy — we can't stress this enough. You can add it as a creamy protein-rich sauce to a wrap, or use it as a base and combine with lemon juice, lemon zest, caper juice, and capers to make a simple vegan caesar dressing.

INGREDIENTS

2 cups garbanzo beans
1 tablespoon tahini
1 teaspoon cumin
2 pieces garlic
2 tablespoons lemon juice
1 teaspoon salt
½ cup oil

CHEFFING INSTRUCTIONS

- Add ingredients to blender and pulverize.
- Add additional oil until hummus achieves desired consistency.

PAIRING SUGGESTIONS

Toss in roasted red peppers, kalamata olives, or sundried tomatoes to take this hummus to the next level.
Pita bread or cucumbers.

SLAW

THE DISH: It's our adamant belief that you should add slaw to everything: tacos, burgers, salads, etc. Generally speaking, you can toss any kind of vegetables together for slaw, even broccoli and cauliflower, and toss with some light salt, sugar, vinegar, and citrus juice.

INGREDIENTS

2 tablespoons lime juice
1 tablespoon vinegar
1 teaspoon salt
1 teaspoon sugar

¼ cabbage
1 carrot, peeled
½ cup fresh cilantro, diced
½ cucumber, sliced length-wise, seeded

CHEFFING INSTRUCTIONS

• Thinly slice cabbage, and grate carrots.
• Once the cucumber has been seeded, slice into thin quarter-moons.
• Add cabbage to a mixing bowl with salt, and knead by hand.
Then add remaining vegetables, cilantro, sugar, lime juice, and vinegar, and stir together thoroughly.

← SLAW ON EVERYTHING →

PICKLED ONIONS (OR CARROTS, OR WHATEVS)

THE DISH: A simple pickled onion garnish can go a long way in terms of making dishes look classy AF. You can add pickled onions to salads, tacos, burgers, or whatever, but you've gotta eat with your pinkies up.

INGREDIENTS

2 onions, sliced thin
1 cup apple cider vinegar

2 tablespoons sugar
3 teaspoons salt
~2 cups hot water

CHEFFING INSTRUCTIONS

- Slice onions thin.
- In a container, add onions, then top with sugar, salt, and vinegar. Top with hot water until onions are completely submerged.
- Allow onions to cool for an hour before refrigerating.

SUGGESTIONS

You can also pickle carrots or other vegetables this way. It's quick and easy, and you can refrigerate them and store the pickled veggies for later.

← PICKLED ONIONS ON EVERYTHING →

HOT SAUCE

THE DISH: Once you make your own hot sauce, you'll never go back to store-bought swill. Hot sauce is super easy to make, and really only requires two key components: xanthan gum (for consistency, so it's not a watery mess), and a decent blender.

HOT SAUCE BASE

~2 cups of hot peppers of your choosing
1 cup water
½ cup white vinegar
2 teaspoons celery salt
1 teaspoon sugar
¼ teaspoon xanthan gum (stirred with 2 tablespoons water, and allowed to sit)

CHEFFING TIPS

• We roast the peppers so they acquire a slightly smoky, charred taste.
• On top of the base, you can get creative and add things like lime juice, tequila, smoked paprika, lime zest, cilantro, canned chipotles, or whatever else you feel would make the sauce diabolical.
• Blend everything together, completely pulverizing it. Then add the xanthan gum/water mixture and pulverize a second time. Allow hot sauce to sit for an hour before refrigerating. With the vinegar, the hot sauce will last for up to a month.

CHEEZE SPREAD FIRST ON TACOS!

THE DISH: There's no recipe here. This is more of a lesson culled from life as to how to organize a taco the proper way. This is 30+ years of learned taco-eating experience. It's not dissimilar from acknowledging that there is a correct way to assemble a sandwich: bottom bun—patty—cheeze—fixin's.

Here is the life-hack for tacos: put a cheeze spread as the first layer of the taco, then add the base like seasoned "beef," or carnitas, or walnut chorizo, or whatnot. The spread acts as a glue and keeps the base from sliding off the tortilla.

HOW TO LAYER A TACO:

1. TORTILLA

2. CHEEZE SPREAD

3. FIXINS

4. SLAW, SALSA, AIOLI

SUNDRIED TOMATOES

THE DISH: Sundried tomatoes cost a million dollars at grocery stores and we have no idea why. It's un-democratic is what it is.

SUNDRIED TOMATOES RECIPE

~8 roma tomatoes
~5 pieces garlic
1 tablespoon oregano
1 cup oil

CHEFFING INSTRUCTIONS

• Slice the tomatoes in half, top-to-bottom.
• Arrange on a pan, lightly sprinkle with salt, and bake at 350° for a half-hour. Remove the pan from oven. Using a spatula, flatten the tomatoes so that the juice releases. Either flip the tomatoes or continue baking for an additional half-hour until tomatoes are lightly blackened.
• In a container, add tomatoes, garlic, oregano, and then cover with oil. Add water to completely submerge tomatoes.

The Trail's End Saloon

They were somewhere around Zion, on the edge of the desert, when the Ring Pops began to take hold.

Jean-Claude van Randy, Speed Dog, and Rach found themselves reposed on a bench outside the Trail's End Saloon, facing the long, dusty road headed out of town. In the distance was the great beyond and no sign of a plant-based watering hole for as far as the eye could see.

Faced with the inevitability of being a hungry vegan on the road, Randy suggested they find something to eat before skipping town. "Don't know when we'll happen upon the next plant-based watering hole."

Speed Dog crushed a Ring Pop in his teeth in response; his sunglasses jostled on the bridge of his nose like an angry toddler.

"I need some air conditioning before I get back in that van," Rach chimed in, clad in her signature black jeans, black faux-leather jacket, and black sunglasses.

The bartender at the Trail's End Saloon suggested the vegan banh mi, featuring house-made banh "meat."

Randy chuckled; Speed Dog bit into another Ring Pop. They were happy to have found anything vegan-friendly, expecting Trail's

End to be another slimy-portabella-mushroom-cap-and-half-ass-hummus type of venue. The walls were flush with knockoff Georgia O'Keeffe's and maps of the Old West; the seats were set with steak knives, and the condiments selection was a bouquet of variations on A1.

An hour later and the crew sidled into the Aerostar touring van.

Speed Dog turned to Randy as he angled the Aerostar onto the road with precision: his drum-solo. "That bar-hand was right," he said. "That sammy should run for president — I'd vote for it."

The bar-hand stood on the dusty patio outside the Trail's End Saloon, watching the Aerostar glide off into the distance.

Footsteps announced the arrival of the bar-hand's compatriot, the chef. "Who were those guys?" the chef asked. "Rockstars?"

"Something like that," the bar-hand said.

The sound of footsteps on the wooden planks as the chef shuffled away.

The bar-hand took one last long look; the Aerostar was but a speck of shimmering quicksilver on the horizon. "Vegan rockstars," he said, to no one and to nothing. ∎

FIN

Index

CHEEZES

DESSERTS

DRESSING & SAUCES

SIDES

VEGGIE-BASED MEAT SUBSTITUTES

VEGAN "MEATS"

Recipes

ERIC OBENAUF is the Editorial Director of Two Dollar Radio, a press he founded with his wife, Eliza. Eric was included in *Publishers Weekly*'s "50 Under 40" list, spotlighting 50 individuals working in publishing under age 40 worth watching, and was one of five (5) finalists in the magazine's 2016 "Star Watch" awards.

At Two Dollar Radio Headquarters, Eric stocks the books and chefs it up in the kitchen. He enjoys camping, hiking, reading outside with a beer or two like a gentleman, and dad jokes.